Medical Miracles

Andy McPhee

SCHOLASTIC INC.

New York   Toronto   London   Auckland   Sydney
Mexico City   New Delhi   Hong Kong   Buenos Aires

Cover
© **Digital Vision**

Developed by ONO Books in cooperation with Scholastic Inc.

ISBN 0-439-59793-5

12 13 14 15 16 17   23   12 11 10 09 08

Contents

Welcome to This Book

Do you ever think about what your heart does? What about your liver, your skin, your bones, or your ears?

Most people don't. But all that changes when something goes wrong. Each teen in this book had a terrible health emergency. And each one pulled through with a lot of help from medical science.

How did they beat the odds? What did doctors do to help these kids? Read on to discover the true stories behind seven medical miracles.

Target Words These words help describe the amazing ways that doctors can help people.

- **donate:** to give something as a gift

  Kaylee got a new heart because someone decided to donate one.

- **injury:** damage or bodily harm, including cuts, bruises, and broken bones

  Adam suffered a bad injury playing football and had to be carried off the field.

- **ordeal:** a very difficult or painful experience

  John survived a terrible accident and wrote a book about his ordeal.

Reader Tips Here's how to get the most out of this book.

- **Chapter Titles** Chapter titles give you a clue about the main idea of each chapter. For instance, in Chapter 2, "Lending an Ear," the information will be about ears and hearing.

- **Cause/Effect** The cause makes something happen. Ask yourself "Why?" to find the cause. An effect is what happens. Ask yourself "What happened?" to find the effect. Understanding cause and effect will help you make sense of what you read.

1

Standing Tall

Would football star Adam Taliaferro ever walk again?

In September 2000, Adam Taliaferro was playing football for Pennsylvania State University. There was a minute and a half left in the game. The other team had the ball. Adam dove at the ball carrier and tackled him headfirst. His **opponent** got up. Adam did not.

Adam wanted to stand up and walk back to the huddle. But he couldn't feel his legs. He wanted to push himself up with his arms. He couldn't.

Adam felt confused—and scared. Why couldn't he move? Around him, all play had stopped. Team doctor Wayne Sebastianelli and his assistants ran onto the field. "It was clear the moment I saw him that he had a spinal cord **injury**," said Dr. Sebastianelli.

The spinal cord is a long bundle of nerves. It stretches from the brain to the bottom of the spine. It carries signals from the brain to the body and back. When the spinal cord is hurt, those signals may be blocked. If the signals can't get through, the brain can't tell the muscles to move.

That is what happened to Adam. He couldn't move. He was **paralyzed.**

Emergency Aid

Adam had to be kept as still as possible. Any movement could cause more damage. The medical team carefully strapped Adam to a special board. They didn't even remove his helmet. Then they sped to the medical center.

Doctors X-rayed Adam right away. They found he had broken a bone in his neck. The bones in the neck and down the spine are called **vertebrae.** They protect the spinal cord.

Adam had broken the fifth bone from the top. His spinal cord had also been cut near the broken bone. That was bad news. It meant that Adam might be paralyzed from the neck down. The doctors had to act fast.

First, the doctors gave Adam a drug to bring down the swelling. That's because swelling can squeeze nerve cells and damage them even more.

Next, Adam needed an operation. The doctors explained that it was a serious operation. But Adam told them to go ahead. He was not ready to give up. He told his mother, "I'm not going out like this."

In the operating room, doctors **fused** part of Adam's spine in place. They screwed a steel plate to two vertebrae in his neck. The plate would lock the bones together and keep them from moving. That would help protect the spinal cord so Adam could heal.

Back to Life

Doctors had hope for Adam. They knew he had gotten treatment fast. They also knew his spinal cord hadn't been cut all the way through. That meant that some of the nerves were still connected. The doctors felt that there was a chance that Adam might be able to walk again one day. But only time would tell.

For several days, Adam could only move his eyes and mouth. Then, something amazing happened. Adam wiggled the big toe on his left foot. It was a hopeful sign. But doctors warned him that he was still a long way from walking.

Adam worked with **physical therapists.** They helped him do exercises to rebuild his strength.

Little by little, Adam got movement back in his arms and legs. He worked hard. He was determined to get back on his feet.

Three months after his injury, Adam Taliaferro walked out of the hospital. All he had for help were crutches.

In September 2001, Adam returned to the football field. His playing days were over. But that day his teammates honored him. He led the Penn State team onto the field before the game. And he was walking all by himself. There were no crutches in sight. That was the biggest victory of his life.

Heads Up!

How did doctors respond to Adam's injury? List what they did, in order.

Courtesy Penn State Sports

Adam Taliaferro led the Penn State football team across a field before a game—without crutches!

Wired for Movement

You scratch your nose. You pick up a pencil. You cross your legs. Have you ever wondered how your body can do all these things? It all starts with the brain.

Your brain generates a signal, such as "scratch itchy nose." The signal is called a nerve **impulse.** And it travels along the spinal cord.

All along the spinal cord, there are bunches of nerves that travel to different parts of your body. So the "scratch itchy nose" signal would go into a nerve bundle that led to one of your arms. Then it would go into your hand, and finally into one of your fingers. Take that, itchy nose!

But if the spinal cord gets hurt, the signal from your brain can't get through. That's what happened to Adam when he got hurt.

Any injury to the spinal cord is bad. But usually, the higher up the injury, the worse it is. If the spinal cord is damaged high in the neck, it may cut off signals to the whole body. If its injury is lower, the legs may be affected but not the upper body.

Adam's injury was pretty high up. That's what makes his story a medical miracle.

2

Lending an Ear

Can science help a deaf girl hear?
And will she want to?

Alicia Helfert was born deaf. She had never heard a dog bark. She had never heard a song on the radio. She had never heard the sound of her mother's voice.

Alicia coped well without hearing. As a young child, she learned sign language. That's a way to communicate using hand gestures. Her family and friends learned it, too.

But as the years went by, scientists learned more about how the ear works. They came up with new ideas about how to help people hear. A new **device** for hearing was invented.

The tiny device has two parts. One part is **implanted** under the skin behind the ear. The other part is worn outside the ear.

Courtesy Alicia Helfert

Alicia was born deaf. She couldn't hear music or her family's voices. But medical science changed all that.

Pump Up the Volume

The device acts like a microphone. It picks up sound waves and changes them to electrical signals. The signals are sent to nerves in a part of the ear called the cochlea (KOH-klee-eh). That's why the device is called a cochlear implant.

Cochlear implants don't work for all deaf people. They only work if the implant can replace the part of the ear that is not working properly. If another part of the ear is damaged, then the implant won't help.

Even when the implant works, the sound is not completely natural. Some people have described the sound as tinny or "robotlike." That's because the implant can't transmit sounds exactly the way a working ear does. Still, the implant can make a big difference. It can turn a silent world into one that's full of sound.

A Tough Choice

The doctors told Alicia that she could be helped by the implant. But Alicia had to think about it. First of all, any operation is risky and there is always the possibility that something could go wrong. Another thing Alicia had to consider was that sometimes the implants don't work well enough to help a person hear clearly.

But Alicia had even more to think about. People who are deaf communicate in their own language. This language, called signing, gives the deaf community a strong **identity.** Some deaf people feel that those who choose implants are turning their backs on who they really are.

That's how some of Alicia's friends felt. "When I finally decided to get one," said Alicia, "the deaf kids picked on me. It was a really hard decision."

But Alicia stuck with her decision. She got the implant in 2000, when she was fourteen years old. At first, she found it hard to get used to. Imagine if everyone around you suddenly started speaking a strange language. That's what it's like when a deaf person hears sound for the first time.

Heads Up!

Alicia's friends didn't like that she decided to get the implant. Why? Do you agree with her friends? Why or why not?

The first sound Alicia heard was her mother's voice. After that, she remembers hearing a strange rumbling sound. She had no clue what it was. It turned out to be the washing machine.

Alicia had flushed a toilet thousands of times. But she had never heard the sound. When she finally did, it scared her.

Now, Alicia has heard laughter, screams, and shouts of joy. Alicia especially loves the sounds of her family's voices. "I can hear them now," she says. "That's a cool sound."

Heads Up!

How has getting the implant changed Alicia's life? What would you have done?

Say What?

Every day, the sounds of the world flood into your ears. You hear phones ringing, friends laughing, and, of course, your favorite music.

How does the ear make that happen?

First, sound waves enter the ear canal. Then, they hit your eardrum. The eardrum is a thin sheet of tissue. It's called the eardrum because it's a lot like the skin of a drum. When sound waves hit the eardrum, it **vibrates.**

Behind the eardrum are three tiny bones. They pass the vibrations on to the cochlea. The cochlea is a spiral of tissue the size of a pea. It's full of tiny nerve **fibers.** The nerve fibers carry the vibrations to the auditory nerve. The auditory nerve picks up the vibrations as signals and sends them to the brain. Then the brain interprets the signals as specific sounds.

For many deaf people, the three bones behind the eardrum don't vibrate normally. It's like a bad connection. So sound waves never make it to the cochlea.

A cochlear implant picks up sound waves and turns them into electrical signals. Then it sends those signals past the eardrum and the tiny bones. They go straight to the cochlea and on to the brain. That's what allowed Alicia to hear.

17

3

Shielded From Disaster

Could doctors "grow" Sean McCormack a new rib cage?

Sean McCormack has always loved sports. He likes to mountain bike. And he was a star pitcher on his Little League baseball team. But there was one big difference between Sean and his friends. Sean risked his life every time he got on a bike or stepped on the pitcher's mound.

Sean was born without a rib cage on the left side of his body. That meant that his heart was unprotected. A blow to the chest could kill him.

Doctors thought they could help Sean. But they wanted to wait until Sean was an adult and his bones had stopped growing. Then they would insert a hard plate into his chest. The plate would protect his heart. Until then, Sean would have to be very careful.

But Sean didn't want to wait. He wanted to play sports without worrying about his health. His parents wanted the same thing for him. So in 1994, they took Sean to Children's Hospital in Boston, Massachusetts. Sean was twelve years old.

What If They Mess Up?

Doctors in Boston wanted to try something completely new. They wanted to build a rib cage inside Sean. Sean's parents liked the idea. But they left the decision up to their son.

Sean admits that he was scared. After all, doctors had never done surgery like this before. "At first, I was like, what if they mess up?" Sean remembers thinking. He says that what he finally did was try to pretend that the operation was no big deal. "I put it in my head that they've done this a million times," he said. With that thought in mind, Sean decided to go for it.

First, the doctors worked outside of Sean's chest. They built a shield out of a special kind of plastic. The shield was about the size of a CD. Doctors molded it into the shape of the missing part of Sean's rib cage.

Before Sean got his cartilage shield, a fall on his mountain bike might have killed him.

Doctors then scraped some cartilage cells from Sean's breastbone. Cartilage is part of the **skeletal** system and is almost as hard as bone. The doctors planted the cells on the plastic shield and added special growth cells. Then they waited for the cells to grow. They were hoping that the cells would grow into cartilage.

It worked! Sean's cells grew into cartilage and the cartilage covered the plastic shield. It was time for the operation. The doctors put the shield inside Sean's chest and hoped for the best.

Sean's body did exactly what doctors had hoped it would do. Within a year, the plastic part was gone. Sean's body broke it down. Only cartilage remained. It was as though Sean had grown his own shield for his heart.

Today Sean is six feet tall. His shield has grown along with him. "It's pretty cool," says Sean about his cartilage shield. "It looks like something I was born with."

Heads Up!

How do you think Sean's life is different now that he has a cartilage shield?

The Bare Bones

Touch the tip of your nose. Now touch the top part of your ears. That's cartilage. When you were born, your body had over 300 pieces of it. During the first months of your life, most of your cartilage hardened into bone. Some of these bones fused together. So, today you should have a grand total of 206.

Bones are the toughest things in your body. Some are as hard as rock. But inside, they're soft and spongy. They're filled with capillaries and a soft material called marrow. Marrow works as a blood factory. It makes red blood cells.

Bones have two main functions. They hold you up, and they protect your organs. Imagine what might happen to your brain if you had no skull. Imagine what might happen to your heart and lungs without ribs.

You have 12 pairs of ribs—that's 24 bones. They all attach to your spine. The top seven pairs also attach to your sternum, or breast bone. Without a rib cage on the left side, Sean's heart was **vulnerable.**

His doctors couldn't grow bone, but they could grow cartilage. It's not quite as strong as bone, but it was a medical miracle. And it did the trick.

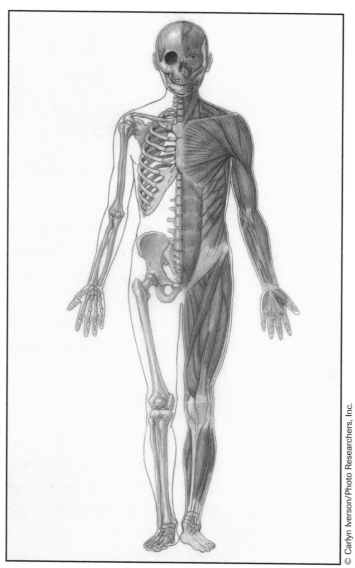

Without your bones, your muscles and flesh would be in a pile on the floor.

© Carlyn Iverson/Photo Researchers, Inc.

4

Limb From Limb

After losing his arms in a terrible accident,
John Thompson needed a miracle.

On January 11, 1992, John Thompson was working on his family's farm in North Dakota. The eighteen-year-old was about to unload some bins of grain. Suddenly, his shirt got caught in a piece of farm machinery. The machine spun John around five or six times. Then it threw him to the ground.

John was knocked out. He woke up a few minutes later. His dog Tuffy was licking his face. But as soon as John awoke, he knew something was terribly wrong. "I couldn't feel my left arm," John later remembered. "I couldn't see my right arm. I went to pick myself up and my arms were gone. I thought I was going to die."

Getting Help

Both of John's arms had been ripped off at the shoulders. He knew he needed help right away. But he was alone on the farm. Somehow, John got to his feet and stumbled to the house. There, he opened the door with his mouth.

John tried to dial the phone with his nose. When that didn't work, he picked up a pencil with his teeth. He used the pencil to punch the numbers on the phone and call for help. Then he climbed into the bathtub to wait for an ambulance to arrive. He didn't want to drip blood on his mother's clean carpet.

John was not sure he would live until help arrived. He thought he might bleed to death in the tub. But when the body suffers a severe injury like John's, it tries to save itself. In John's case, the blood vessels in his shoulders tightened. The tightening slowed the flow of blood.

John was alive and conscious when the ambulance crew got to his house. He told the emergency medical worker where to find his arms. They wrapped his arms in garbage bags and packed them in ice. They hoped the ice would keep the cells alive. If it worked, doctors might be able to sew John's arms back on.

Saving John's arms was important. But saving his life was the first thing doctors thought about. By the time John got to the emergency room, he had lost about half his blood. Right away, doctors gave John blood and other fluids through a vein.

Next, doctors rushed John to an operating room to work on his arms. Every moment counted. The severed limbs were cut off from John's blood supply. Without blood, the tissue in his arms would begin to die.

The **surgeons** worked as fast as they could. They used screws to reattach the bones. Then they worked on the smaller parts of the arms. They used microscopes and tiny tools to connect the blood vessels and nerves. Once this was done, the surgeons stitched John's muscles and skin back together. Altogether, the operation took six hours.

Heads Up!
What happened after John arrived at the hospital? Retell the events in your own words.

© C. Mike Malone/Mutual of Omaha

Thanks to medical science, John can hold his dog Tuffy in his arms.

John had a long way to go after the operation. He went through months of physical therapy so he could learn to use his arms again. One of the things he did was lift light weights to make his muscles stronger.

John's recovery was amazing. He still doesn't have full control over his hands and fingers, but his arms function fairly well.

Today, John travels around the country. He speaks to people who want to hear his story. He has also written a book about his **ordeal** called *Home in One Piece*.

John hopes his story will help other people who face personal tragedies. "Each one of us," he says, "can do more than we ever dreamed of doing."

Heads Up!

Why did John write a book about his accident? Do you think you would have done the same thing if you were him?

The Beat Goes On

Put your hand on your throat. Next to where you swallow you can feel a pulsing.

That's your circulatory system at work. With each beat of your heart, blood is pushed through your body.

The heart is a muscular organ located behind the rib cage. It's about the size of a clenched fist and is divided into two pumps.

One pump takes in blood from the body and sends it to the lungs. There, the blood is enriched with oxygen. The other pump receives oxygen-rich blood from the lungs and sends it back out to the body.

A system of blood vessels called arteries carry blood away from the heart. Tiny blood vessels called capillaries deliver oxygen-rich blood to every point in your body.

Cells need oxygen to live. That's why doctors had to work so fast to sew John's arms back on.

After blood has delivered oxygen to your cells, another system of blood vessels called veins carries it back to the heart.

Then the cycle begins again. Blood circulates through the entire body in about one minute.

5

She's Got Heart

Kaylee Davidson needed a new heart.
But would her body reject it?

Kaylee Davidson likes to listen to music. She likes to hang out with her friends. And she hates to clean her room. Kaylee is just like any teenager, right? Well, she's not. But if you met her, you'd never know her secret. Kaylee doesn't have the heart she was born with.

In 1987, Kaylee was the first baby in England to survive a heart **transplant.** When she was five months old, doctors gave Kaylee's parents bad news. Kaylee had a rare kind of heart disease. The disease made it hard for her heart to pump blood. The disease had no cure.

But Kaylee's doctors had a plan. They wanted to remove Kaylee's sick heart and replace it with a heart from another infant who had just died.

At the time, only two other babies in all of England had been given new hearts. Both of those babies had died.

Kaylee's mother, Carol Davidson, was terrified. "It was very, very scary," she recalled later. But the Davidson's had no choice. Without a new heart, Kaylee would die for sure. Doctors said that with a new heart, Kaylee had a fifty-fifty chance of surviving. That was Kaylee's best hope.

A Brand-New Heart

In October 1987, doctors found a heart for Kaylee. An infant had just died. The child's parents wanted to help other children who needed **organs** to survive. So, they let doctors use the heart for Kaylee.

It took six hours to place the new heart in Kaylee's tiny body. Everything went just the way it was planned. But for heart transplant patients, getting through surgery isn't the only worry.

The body has its own security force called the immune system. Its job is to keep you safe from disease. When your immune system finds germs in your body, it attacks them.

The problem is, the immune system does the same thing to a strange organ. So, Kaylee has to take medicine to keep her immune system from attacking her heart. But these drugs don't always work. When that happens, there's only one thing to do. The patient has to get a new transplant. And it has to happen fast.

The Kaylee Plan

Kaylee was lucky. The drugs worked for her. But they keep her immune system weak. That means it has trouble fighting off germs. So Kaylee has to watch closely for any sign of a cold, flu, or other infection. If she thinks she's getting sick, she goes to the doctor right away.

Her teachers, friends, and parents watch her closely, too. Kaylee's school even has a "Kaylee Plan," in case anything goes wrong.

—Heads Up!—
Kaylee's drugs keep her body from attacking her heart. But they also have a harmful side effect. What is it?

With her new heart, Kaylee can now do everything that other kids can do.

One day when Kaylee was thirteen, she had chest pains while she was at school. The school called an air ambulance to get her. A helicopter landed on the school playground. It took Kaylee off to the hospital.

But for the most part, Kaylee doesn't think her life is unusual. "I wouldn't say I was different," she said. "I do everything that everyone else does."

For that, she's incredibly grateful. She gives talks all over England urging people to become organ donors. "If it wasn't for organ donors," said Kaylee, "I wouldn't be here today. They give people like me a chance to live."

Heads Up!

Reread "The Beat Goes On" on page 29. Then look at the diagram of the heart on page 35. What does the heart do?

The Heart of the Matter

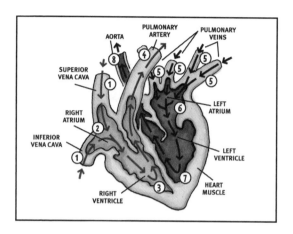

How does your heart work, anyway?

1. Blood from the body enters the heart from two large veins: the **inferior vena cava** and the **superior vena cava.**
2. The blood then accumulates in the **right atrium.**
3. Next, the blood passes into the **right ventricle.**
4. Then, the blood moves into the **pulmonary artery** to the lungs. In the lungs, blood receives oxygen.
5. The oxygen-rich blood then moves into the **pulmonary veins.** (There are two pulmonary veins from each lung.)
6. Next, the blood moves into the **left atrium.**
7. It then travels into the **left ventricle.**
8. The oxygen-rich blood is pumped back into the body through an artery called the **aorta.**

6

Third Time's a Charm

**Destin Wright needed a new liver—fast.
Would doctors be able to beat the clock?**

Destin Wright was nine years old the first time the whites of his eyes turned yellow. The yellow color was a sign of too much bile in Destin's blood. Bile is a substance produced by the liver. It helps break down food in the body.

Yellow eyes meant that something was wrong with Destin's liver. Three years later doctors discovered that Destin had a liver condition called cirrhosis (sir-OH-sis).

"We were told he had less than a year to live," recalled his mother, Lori Wright.

Destin's only chance of survival was a liver transplant. He needed an organ from a donor. But not just any liver would do. It would have to be a good match.

A new liver gave Destin a chance to celebrate graduation with his sister.

Courtesy Lori Wright

To find a good match, the first thing doctors do is test for blood type. About half of all people are type O. The rest are types A, B, and AB.

Both the donor and the person getting the liver need to have the same blood type. Then they try to match the tissue, using other tests. They can never be sure they have a perfect match. But they try to get as close as possible.

This process can take a long time. Destin couldn't wait. So his doctors asked his mother, Lori, to **donate** a piece of her liver. That's called a live-donor transplant. It's special because most transplants come from donors who have died.

In a live-donor transplant, doctors take out part of a healthy person's liver. They transplant it into the body of the sick person. Then they wait for a miracle. The liver is the only organ inside the body that can regrow itself. The transplant can grow to normal size within eight weeks.

Heads Up!

Look up donate *in the glossary. Name other ways a person can donate to a good cause.*

Tests showed that Lori's liver was a good match for her son's. Would she donate part of her liver? It would be painful and risky. But Lori didn't think twice. "I didn't blink about it," she said.

Back From Death's Door

At first, after the operation, both mother and son recovered well. But the excitement didn't last long. After two weeks, Destin's body started rejecting his new liver.

Destin was lucky. His surgeons were able to find another donor quickly. But the second transplant lasted only a year. During that time, Destin never felt totally well. Finally, his body rejected the second liver, too.

Now Destin was in big trouble. He was sick and weak. At fifteen years old, he weighed just ninety pounds. But his surgeons finally managed to find a third liver.

Destin had his third liver transplant in January 2002. The new liver made a big difference. And Destin hasn't looked back since. "I'm fine now," he says. "I'm always on the go."

What a Workhorse

The liver is like a factory with a big filter. Blood flows through the liver constantly. The liver filters the blood. At the same time, it makes important chemicals. Here are the liver's main jobs:

- removing waste and other poisons from the blood

- keeping a balance of **hormones** in the blood

- producing red blood cells and platelets (needed for blood to clot)

- storing glucose (sugar) and releasing it when it's needed for energy

- making proteins that help the blood clot

- making bile, which helps break down food

- making cholesterol, a type of fat that helps cells maintain their shape

People can get cirrhosis from diseases that harm the liver. But poisons, such as alcohol, also harm the liver and lead to cirrhosis. Destin's condition was something he was born with. Luckily, his ordeal ended with a medical miracle.

7

Into the Fire

No one thought Gavin Sweezie would survive. But he did.

Gavin Sweezie was fourteen. He was looking forward to a great vacation. He and his family lived in British Columbia, Canada. They were driving their motor home all the way to California. They were going to visit Disneyland, and Gavin was excited.

The family never made it. Their motor home crashed into a large truck. The motor home burst into flames. Gavin's mother, sister, and stepfather were killed. Only Gavin survived the explosion.

"It's a miracle he's alive," said one doctor.

Over 80 percent of Gavin's body was burned. Only his wrists and parts of his face and head escaped the fire. Doctors felt certain that Gavin would die, too.

Laid Bare

Gavin was in serious danger. With so much of his skin burned away, his body had no protection against germs.

Everyone's skin has two layers. The top layer protects the tissue underneath. The lower layer contains nerves, blood vessels, sweat glands, and hair. When the lower layer is damaged, germs from the air can get right into the blood. This makes it very hard to fight infection.

Gavin's problem was that both layers of skin were destroyed over most of his body. He had no protection at all.

Doctors got to work as quickly as they could. They gave Gavin antibiotics. An antibiotic is a drug that fights infection. The antibiotics helped Gavin's body resist germs. Without those drugs, he might not have survived.

Heads Up!

Why did Gavin's serious burns put him in so much danger? How does the skin help protect the body?

Today, Gavin works as a volunteer firefighter.

Growing Skin

The next task was to rebuild Gavin's skin. Doctors cut away burned tissue. The process was painful for Gavin. But cleaning away burned tissue allowed healthy tissue to grow in its place.

Still, Gavin's body couldn't grow all the skin it needed on its own. Doctors performed operations called skin grafts to replace the burned skin. In a skin graft, a very thin slice of a patient's healthy skin is removed. The skin is then placed over a burned area. It grows there permanently.

Gavin didn't have much healthy skin to work with. But doctors actually grew new skin for him in a lab. Here's how. First, they removed a small square of Gavin's healthy skin. Then, they placed that skin in a special solution that allowed it to grow new cells. In three weeks doctors had enough skin to cover Gavin's entire body.

Gavin went through a terrible time. He lost three of his closest family members. Then he suffered through months of painful operations. But he's grateful to be alive. He lives in British Columbia, where he grew up. In his spare time, he works as a volunteer firefighter.

More Than Skin Deep

You probably only think about your skin when it doesn't look right. Maybe you've got a dry patch. Maybe you've got a pimple or two. Maybe you've got an itchy, red rash.

But there's more to your skin than how it looks. It's actually an organ, just like your heart or your lungs. In fact, it's your body's biggest organ. And while you're checking yourself out in the mirror, your skin is hard at work keeping you alive.

Every square inch contains two hundred sweat glands and six feet of blood vessels. Stretch it all out and you could cover a twin bed. But that's not all. Your skin has two layers. The top layer is called the epidermis. That's the part you see. Under that is the dermis. That's the part you don't see unless you're hurt.

Your skin protects your body from germs. It also controls your body's temperature. It helps keep heat in when you're cold. And it cools you down with sweat when you're hot.

It also helps get rid of waste (through sweat). And it provides a cushion for all the bumps and bruises your body takes.

So next time you get mad at your skin, just think of where you'd be without it.

Glossary

device *(noun)* a machine designed to do a specific job (p. 12)

donate *(verb)* to give something as a gift (p. 38)

fiber *(noun)* a thin, threadlike structure (p. 17)

fuse *(verb)* to join together (p. 8)

hormone *(noun)* a chemical in the body that controls a body function, such as growth (p. 40)

identity *(noun)* the way you define or describe who you are (p. 15)

implant (verb) to place inside (p. 12)

impulse *(noun)* a message that travels along a nerve or muscle fiber (p. 11)

injury *(noun)* damage or bodily harm, including cuts, bruises, and broken bones (p. 6)

opponent *(noun)* someone who plays against you in a sport (p. 6)

ordeal *(noun)* a very difficult or painful experience (p. 28)

organ *(noun)* a part of the body that does a particular job (p. 31)

paralyzed *(adjective)* unable to move (p. 7)

physical therapist *(noun)* a person whose job it is to help people recover from injuries that interfere with their ability to move (p. 9)

skeletal *(adjective)* relating to bones (p. 21)

surgeon *(noun)* a doctor who performs operations (p. 26)

transplant *(noun)* an operation that replaces a diseased organ with a healthy one (p. 30)

vertebra *(noun)* one of the bones that make up the spine (p. 7)

vibrate *(verb)* to move back and forth (p. 17)

vulnerable *(adjective)* without protection (p. 22)

Index